This coloring book belongs to _____

ROCKET

BOAT

FERRY

HOT AIR BALLOON

CANOE

PATROL

HELICOPTER

AIRPLANE

TRAM

TRAIN

TAXI

FIRE TRUCK

AMBULANCE

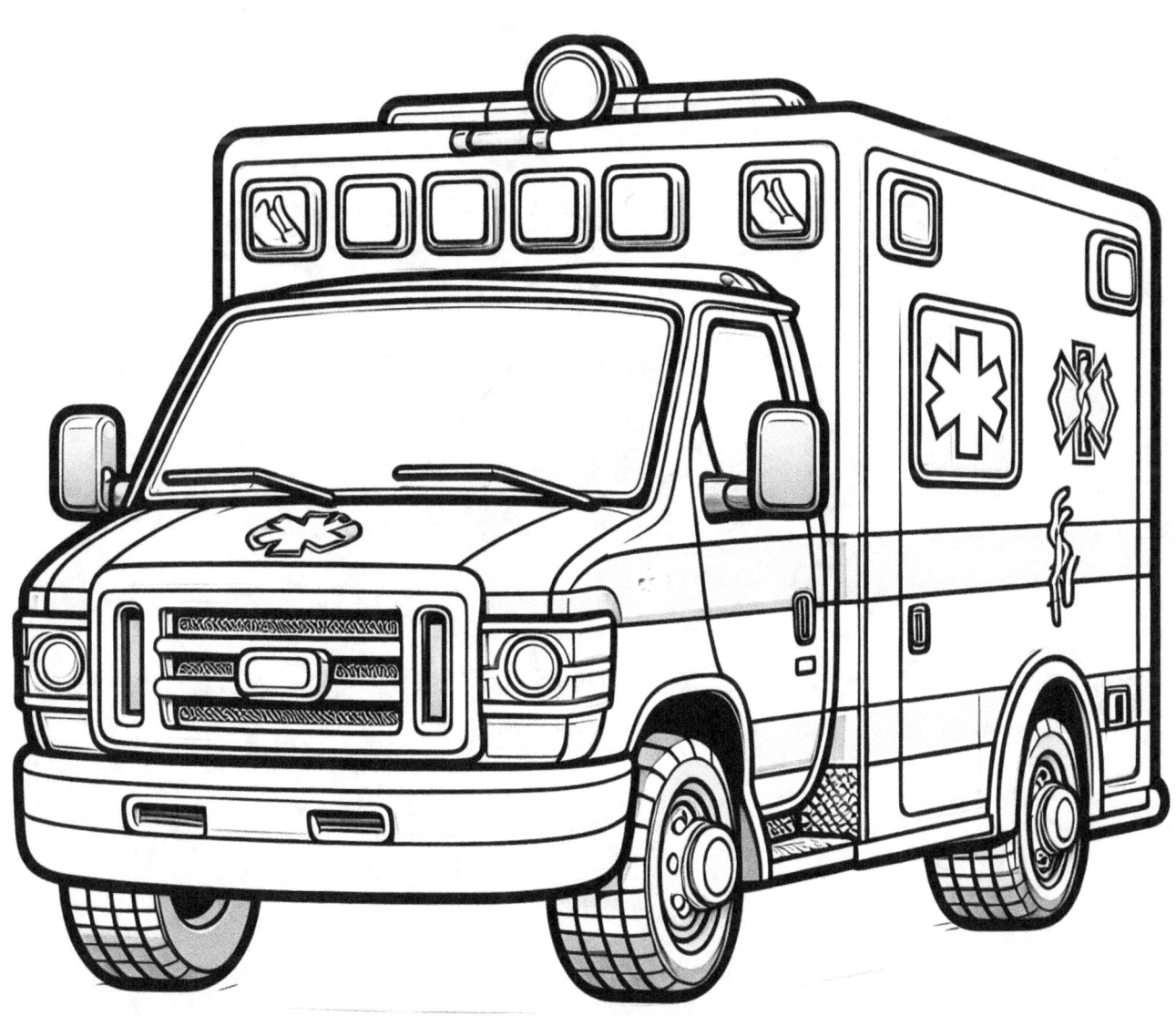

TRACTOR

SCOOTER

TRICYCLE

MOTORCYCLE

BICYCLE

BUS

SUBMARINE

TRUCK

GARBAGE TRUCK

CAR

WAR TANK

RACING MOTORCYCLE

www.ingramcontent.com/pod-product-compliance
Lightning Source LLC
Chambersburg PA
CBHW082241220526

45479CB00005B/1300